JUL 1 3

Easy Math

Easy Math

POEMS

Lauren Shapiro

WINNER OF THE 2011 KATHRYN A. MORTON PRIZE IN POETRY
SELECTED BY MARIE HOWE

Sarabande Books
LOUISVILLE, KENTUCKY

Managing Editor
Sarabande Books, Inc.
2234 Dundee Road, Suite 200
Louisville, KY 40205

Library of Congress Cataloging-in-Publication Data

Shapiro, Lauren J.
 Easy math : poems / Lauren Shapiro.
    p. cm.
 ISBN 978-1-936747-48-1 (pbk. : alk. paper)
 I. Title.
 PS3619.H35623E27 2013
 811'.6—dc23

                    2012029739

Cover art: *Whirligig*, Multiple Plate Etching by Ray Maseman.

Cover and text design by Kirkby Gann Tittle.

Manufactured in the United States.
This book is printed on acid-free paper.

Sarabande Books is a nonprofit literary organization.

The Kentucky Arts Council, the state arts agency, supports
Sarabande Books with state tax dollars and federal funding
from the National Endowment for the Arts.

for Kevin

and for my parents,
Gene and Susan

CONTENTS

Easy Math

§

§

§

ACKNOWLEDGMENTS

Thank you to the following journals in which some of these poems first appeared, many in altered forms: *32 Poems*, *Connotation Press: An Online Artifact*, *Forklift, Ohio*, *jubilat*, *Locuspoint*, *notnostrums*, *Passages North*, *POOL*, and *Thermos*. Thank you to Ander Monson and *DIAGRAM*/New Michigan Press for publishing *Yo-Yo Logic*, a chapbook in which some of these poems also appeared.

I would like to thank my family, whose support has meant a lot to me during the writing of this manuscript: my parents, Gene and Susan, and my brother Dan and sister Amy. Thank you too to my friends and mentors who have read drafts of this manuscript and offered valuable feedback or other support: Dean Young, Bob Hass, Jim Galvin, Dara Weir, James Tate, Heather June Gibbons, Caryl Pagel, Lauren Haldeman, Adam Fell, Mike Anichini, Emily Pettit, Christine Walker, Melissa Stewart, Dianne Bilyak, and most of all my husband, Kevin González, whose insights have been invaluable. Finally, thank you to Marie Howe and Sarah Gorham for their feedback and encouragement.

FOREWORD

This book is funny. Reading the poems out loud to a friend I had to keep stopping—we were both laughing so much. It was late, he was tired, he had to go. Wait Wait, I'd say, one more, laughing so hard I couldn't read—and he'd settle back into his chair, laughing. Who IS this person, we kept saying.

By the end of it we were wrung out, sated and freshened. Goodbye, goodbye, as he walked down the stairs—the world was strange again, and we were in it—still living, and for more than a few minutes, more alive.

The poet is Lauren Shapiro. She might be a relative of Kafka. (When he read his new stories to friends sometimes *he* couldn't read for laughing.) That's how serious she is about living—and living in the USA right now. Among so many other things, this is a book about waking up in this culture, where roses are named after celebrities and "why is it *in* the car, but *on* the bus?" and "The birds twitter in the trees / and the ghosts of Bambi's mother arrives / dragging a bunch of cans behind her". It's dire; it's ridiculous. Oh rarely has the culture been reflected through such a poetry as this.

A graciousness marks this lively imagination—in relationship to who and what she encounters. ("Are you emancipated? / On Atkins? // Have you checked the categories that apply?") The natural world is animate ("the seasons do their square dance / then fall down exhausted") and un-implicated. ("The snow falls blank as a contract no one / will ever sign"). It's in the mind of our speaker where the correspondences happen—in metaphors and similes that make the world happen twice. ("As I walk home . . . the world looks like / a Brueghel painting and all the trees / are sending off beautiful / little equations into the air"). Energy and joy create these metaphors, and if they are in discourse with postmodern malaise, they almost win the argument. I say almost, because the poems are smart enough not to settle for dumb resolutions.

Lauren Shapiro can downshift from the sublime to the profane and back again in less than five seconds. She can glimpse the mystery of what we might call the big picture, and then narrow her eyes to the quotidian sorrows—this capacity holds a worldview that is radically crisp and compassionate. In a poem called "According to the Magazines, Lindsay Lohan is Very Lonely These Days," Shapiro writes, "What I've learned from Hans Christian Andersen / is that there is a tiny world in each pore of the universe / populated by tiny people who also dream / of larger realities." Then she writes, "In the space between coffee / and lunch lies an expanse as unforgiving / as a cross country bus ride." See what I mean? Easy Math.

—Marie Howe

Easy Math

The Conversation

There is always a woman eating a sandwich.
Today she is large as everything
that wasn't said. It is ham and cheese.
Who cares. You're watching me, she seems
to say. Being alone is unlike a chess move.
It is unlike hanging out at the bowling alley
with Dale Hickey. A hundred stuffed animals
the size of a fist and I can't make the claw catch.
Turkey, says Dale Hickey. The lights
are making turkey shapes all over
the place. Turkey. I heard you.
The woman has finished eating her sandwich
and is on to another one. Now she is tiny
as a shrimp. She is eating the smallest
egg salad sandwich in the world. I think,
Maybe I will speak to her. But she does it first.
I've wanted to talk to you for ages, she says,
but instead I keep eating all these sandwiches.
I know, I say. And I keep going to the bowling alley
with Dale Hickey. It's been hell.

Botanical Garden

Of course there's a rose named Martha Stewart.
A dog with feet delicate as paintbrushes tiptoes

through the Japanese tea garden. An after-hospital
calm reaches its bony fingers around my throat

and tugs. I see the cacti. I touch them.
You blockhead, they say. Yes, I know. I've lived

on the edge of an abyss that doesn't even exist.
Now here I am watching a caretaker push

a quadriplegic's nose into a rosebush. An infant
in a stroller cries. Her mother bends into her like a prayer.

Across town, Happy Hour is just lifting its feet
to tap Billy Joel into the ground. I know, I've waited for it.

Next door in the café old men eat scones
and talk about Iraq. The women at the next table

also talk about Iraq. The children, too, playing in the corner—
they don't know it, but they're talking about Iraq.

The sun is setting. Martha Stewart opens up her petals
like a cup of tea in the jungle. The delicate dog takes

a delicate piss. The quadriplegic smells Martha Stewart.
I smell her. A line starts. Even the infant wants a go.

ESL Students

They ask, Why is it *in* the car but *on* the bus?
I turn up my hands and give them a pained expression.
There is a moment of quiet anger. Then they pop
open their blouses and the buttons fall
like foreign coins to the floor.
They stand on the desks. They kick the air.
We're sick of this bullshit, they say.
I am very still. I look them in the eyes.
We've shown you our tits! they shout.
Yes, I say quietly, and begin to unbutton my cardigan.
The class is silent. For some time we stand there naked,
they on their desks and me in front of the blackboard.
Then Maoki says, There is a different scene
in every room in the world.
Our clothes are but the lint of a passing era, says Hana.
I will light a candle and watch the prayer moths
circle the room like used napkins, says Oui.
I don't speak. A shadow passes over the left
side of my chest. Then the bell rings.

Bent Syllogism

There was a pattern to the way the mythical beasts
flew over the dreary town, but we were too dreary
to understand it. The psychologist, too, was in touch
with extraterrestrials, but she had to stand on the spire
of a church and wear 3-D glasses to see them.
If Amy loves you, then Alice will bake a pie.
But Alice didn't bake a pie.
Therefore, moot point, no pie, no love, nothing.
They say advanced math is like music
but music isn't like advanced math—true—
and yet all third graders in Miss Mathews's class
must learn to play the recorder.
Can't you tell the baby is extremely conflicted?
Can't you see I've lost half a pound?
I write about the polarization of grasses
and the esteemed poet writes how impressed
we are with the polarization of grasses.
Once I'm in my place I start to believe
all the postmodern theories, signs and cosines,
pi, infinity, the artist formerly known as
the artist formerly known as Prince.
I take the symbol out of my pocket, brush it off
and send it on its way. By the time
I get to the gingerbread house I'm ready
to be fooled. The birds twitter in the trees
and the ghost of Bambi's mother arrives,
dragging a bunch of cans behind her.
The children understand this metaphor.
They dance around in a lively pagan ritual.

I have been away for some time.
I don't speak this language anymore.
Please teach me.

What to Do

I begin by painting the nude woman.
She is a cantaloupe in the most famous
still life in history. The world is reflected
in the belly of the nude that shows me only
an ever-repeating image of myself.
I cover one eye with a grape leaf
but I am still there, hunched in a ball
in the belly of the nude woman.
I hear her whispering. Are you speaking
of beauty? I ask. She wants lunch.
We eat the still life next to her.
I can't even get into what happens next.
When I have finished the painting
it hangs in the student show.
A man looks at it. He doesn't know what
to say. I don't know what to say.
It's colorful, he says.
Thanks, I say.

Canis Soupus

On their way to the East Coast, the West Coast coyotes
mated with wolves and dogs. They didn't do it
to improve their species. Who thinks like that?
When I was a girl, the doll with black curls and a lazy eye
had the best ideas because she could see inside her own head.
Sometimes the best thoughts are the simplest and the simplest
actions the most nuanced, like the shifting rock
that buried 33 miners a mile and a half down and showed
there is an infinite number of ways to torture the soul
with hopefulness. In business they say you have to sell yourself,
which is another way of proclaiming your value to the world
in fat letters on an invoice made out to no one.
Says the entrepreneur, Making pixelated hamburgers may seem
like a waste, but think how many times they will be eaten
in virtual restaurants around the world! Everyone has something to say
about love and impermanence and waste, about which is better,
wet or dry food, mutts or pure breeds.
Birds splat on the picture window, but what a view!
The debate shows only two sides, yes or no.
We've engineered all breeds of dog as candidates
for Best in Show. Now what's to show?

A Day in the Life

Entering a plague-ridden Marseilles, Nostradamus saw a woman sewing herself into a shroud. Later, people would speak of the times as *the times* and bow their heads like cattle. They would wipe their faces with fresh blades of grass and whisper to the roly-polys who were squirming now flat now circular in the mud. Nostradamus knew this though it had not happened yet. He calculated the distance between the woman and where air was tiptoeing backwardly into his nose. He reasoned with himself and won the argument. The woman was halfway done with her sewing. She was using a blind-hem stitch that would fall out of style two years later. This and many other things became apparent to Nostradamus all at once. His mind grew cloudy with the weight of his perceptions in a manner with which he was all too familiar. This again, he thought, and hit his right ear with the scroll of paper he had been clutching. All over Marseilles people alive and dead reverberated with the movement. The woman dropped her hand and grew lighter. She had succeeded in sewing the shroud up to her nose. What a beautiful nose, thought Nostradamus.

Rule Book

At the age of ten you will be allowed
in the deep end. 52 inches will get you
on Thunder Mountain. You must be thirteen
with perfect vision to ride all-terrain vehicles.
Please, no unsupervised children. No idiots.
No mentally deranged wantons. We do allow
two siblings for the price of one on Wednesdays.
Eight Young-At-Heart's for the price of seven
on Sunday at 2 p.m. Please understand that
we cannot make exceptions. The rule is
you must be 6'2" with a chiseled profile
and brooding eyes. Size 32-C or larger to get
on the show. We do not accept coupons
or offer refunds. I sympathize
but just came out of surgery myself.
My kid is also sick. Are your eyes
at least two inches apart? We're really looking
for someone with a better sense of the absurd
who is naturally blonde. Don't feel bad,
we accept less than 1% of applicants.
Are you emancipated? On Atkins?
Have you checked all categories that apply?
Please don't call to hear your status.
The process is fully automated, so
you should receive your results in the mail.

Chorus

Back when I was Nicholas at Glendale Community College
begins the second chapter of the memoir.
We start a band. We do trust exercises and Joan falls
on her head. It's not that we're all drunks but that
it's our inalienable right to pursue happiness
and we're utterly lost.
I believe I can fly, sings R. Kelly.
I was born to make you happy, sings Britney.
The chairs in the coffee shop are decorated with cutouts
of coffee mugs. The valve in my heart is full
of cinnamon candies. Back when I was Nicholas
at Glendale Community College, all the posters
were of Homer Simpson smoking dope.
Each umbrella-filled drink at the chi-chi bar
was the smallest holiday you'd ever known.
Raise the banner. Drop your pants.
Pull the curtain for little orphan Annie on a soapbox.
It is her curse to speak only in song, only
to the converted. Tomorrow and tomorrow and tomorrow
opens like the largest dance, like the longest death.
I'm not that innocent, sings Britney.
Baby, Baby, Baby, sings R. Kelly.

They Promised Me a Thousand Years of Peace

The snow falls blank as a contract no one
will ever sign. Getting rid of nothing
is biblical work. When I lick my shadow,
it tastes like the ground and vice versa.
Snorting lines off your college diploma
is a shallow victory, just as crushing something
with a stiletto must say something about scale:
Hey Porky, I'm crushing your tiny love-note
with my stiletto! Yeah, yeah, it's all about
perspective. Getting back to zero is awesome
if you're coming from negative numbers,
but let's not calibrate the quantity of water
in the glass, or the almost theres, or the time
your elbow brushed mine as we passed in the hall
on our way to the A and B team locker rooms.
The way I feel about mathematics bespeaks a love
of theory in which the proposition never
leads to the conclusion. I unpeel the banana
and find a gap-toothed man hungry as hell.
Is it okay to eat the peel? He asks.
This reminds me of an analogy having to do
with clumsiness and a fistful of lucky pennies.
See, you trip on yourself an exact number of times
each day, but who else is counting?

I'll Never Understand It

I read the fable in which a child's nose grows
into a leafless tree. Why leafless?
The seasons do their square dance
then fall down, exhausted.
The thing I want most in the world
arrives in silver wrapping,
but the neighbor boy
steals it from the doorstep.
The movie shows events in rewind,
the leaves jumping
like frogs into branches.
And if you play that record backward
you'll discover—well, I can't tell you.
See, the otter might be
the world's most social animal,
but that's only by our standards.
We know there were thousands of real pirates,
yet we continue to invent new ones.
In other words, we love facts,
but we love lies more if they amuse us.
Picture it: The wild animals dash
through the grass, in the sun,
but they are not joyous.
That's a human construct.

The One Hundreds

First comes the light, then the clattering
of the skeletons as they fall through
the metal grate. It takes a long time
for all one hundred to make it through.
Then the sergeant walks up to me.
Have all the elk skeletons fallen through
the metal grate? Yes, sir, I say.
They've all fallen through.
What about the parakeets? Have all one hundred
been neutered and received their honey baths?
Yes, sir, the parakeets have been neutered
and have received their honey baths.
The cave creatures and the toy poodles
will be waiting, says the sergeant.
I don't mind misting the cave creatures with musk-soap
or shaving the toy poodles and tying on
new ribbons despite their tiny cries of pain.
Nor do I mind peeling back the nails of the muskrats
or administering the small electric shocks
to the crocodiles. A girl must make a living somehow.
It's around three o'clock when the sergeant passes me
at the willow grove. Are you on your way
to the Newborn Infant Sanitarium? he asks.
No, sir, I say calmly. No, I am not.

History Lesson

The dogs look at me with suspicion.
They smell the lingering sympathy
of the recently bereft. I close my eyes
and grandma walks into the room
with a bowl of sucker candies.
Isaac Newton is on the lam again, she says.
The boy has Asperger's. In our fairytale
I stroke his hair on a beautiful bluff
overlooking the Mississippi. We watch
the maidens doing wash below us, singing
their sad songs. This is how I feel
in Newton's world: alone in a crowd
of blind people chatting.
The trained dogs circle me like sharks.
They know my secret. Later I ask Isaac
why we must always meet
at these blind people parties.
I can't be found out, he says.
He is very hypochondriacal.
I could never tell my grandmother
about our relationship.
Instead I take a pineapple sucker candy.
That's my favorite, too, she says,
and opens the blinds to let the sun in.

The Life of Birds

The first mammals in New Zealand were humans.
How did they survive? They must have eaten birds.

Would I be a genius if I really got it? If the math equation
became the never-ending movie of my life.

Don't let me love something I don't understand.
Don't try to stop me from falling in love, you bastard!

When I went swimming in the lake the swans came.
They're the love birds but they're so fat
they can only land on water.

Does that mean something?

My parakeet with clipped wings loved the piano.
I didn't love the piano or the parakeet,
but I wanted to.

Wanting to be a genius is wanting to fall in love
with someone very far away. You can write long letters
to each other every Sunday over coffee.

In November the hummingbirds begin their journey
across the Gulf of Mexico. Not all of them will survive.

Fly, fly, red-throated hummingbird! Don't stop!
There's so much nectar waiting for you in the Yucatán!

Learning Curve

The couple in the airport break their embrace
and touch elbows like two cranes in a mating dance.
The difference between sexy and sex is larger
than a high school football field. It is emptier
than a hotel gym on Friday night.
When I bite into the apple, it tastes like apple.
Like most inanimate things you see
before you touch: unsurprising.
The blind man dreams a fifth dimension in his sleep.
That is color. That is what happens
when you don't follow the assembly instructions:
someone loses an eye.
Jealousy makes as much sense as pretending
to be blind. Do you learn something
or do you just stub your toe?
Everything I ever needed to know I learned
not-at-all. Everything you ever needed to know
you learned watching that couple kiss.
Step away from the dotted red line!
Take off your headphones when passing through
the metal detector. Please disengage
the fake hip, sir. No extension cords allowed.
No masticating. The music in the terminal
is exceptional. The apple in my pocket
is excited to see you.
Lt. Cmdr. Edward Henry "Butch" O'Hare,
how many women whisper your name
as they climb into bed with their husbands,
imagining the twin turbine engines

beginning their slow and steady rumble?
Lt. Cmdr., did you invent takeoff?
How did you feel when the wheels left the ground?

Hotel

I walk in only to find the 10th Annual
Chicago Bears Fan Convention.
My brain aches from the torment
of never aching like this before.
I came looking for peace but found a panel discussion
on the aerodynamics of jock straps.
Trickledown economics, do your work!
Spread your wings, Sweet Sue.
Blow your blowtorch, Angry Al.
Bastard Barb, keep crying into your napkins
and throwing them under the table. The pile is like
all the fans drinking beer and hugging each other
in the lobby. Light as a shadow of themselves, they rise
to the 16th floor. They refill their ice buckets.
I'm in the hot tub when I get bumrushed
by Tank Johnson. He's wearing a speedo
designed by the Swedish military.
They have a military? I ask.
I just bumrushed you, says Tank Johnson.
Then he leaves to swim laps in the pool.
He's faster than I would have thought.

Is There a Moral to the Story?

Some people say the sun rises and rises and never sets.
I have seen their backs as they follow the rollicking ponies
into the meadow. All is new and foolhardy for them.
Recycling hasn't been invented yet, it's just a blip
on the typewriter ribbon of the future. In other words,
you'll pay for all this later, kids.
And thus the fairytales teach: Be patient. Suffer.
Make sure it's really your grandmother under the covers.
At six, it seemed so easy to climb into the Ice Queen's
jeweled sleigh, but how hard (impossible, even?)
to climb out. The saying goes the dream shattered
or the clock struck twelve. In other words,
you've got it good kids—now go to bed.
Reality is only what we expect to see
come true. On T.V., the 21-year-olds down jello shots,
strap on their heels. And in that pie? Apples, yeah.
All is mayhem in a club on the Jersey Shore
and somewhere far away a war goes click clack
like a toy train you can only hear stuttering and shaking
as it jumps its tracks.

It Makes Philosophical Sense

Most accidents occur in traffic jams.
Or, to put it another way,
it's easier to run into someone
if you're standing two feet away.
I learned about solar wind
next to a ten-year-old in the science museum.
Then he popped his gum in my face and moved on.
Once I knew what it was, I conjured
the largest geomagnetic storm and told it
to do my bidding, but it had more scientific
motivations. It's not hard to teach
an old dog new tricks, it's just hard to get him
to care enough to learn. All along, I've said
you were the best one for the job
of International Earthquake Arbitrator.
Now who are the sides again?
The sundial works from every angle,
but this is not true of most things.
The withered carnation blows across the street
like an old lady's flap of skin, dyed yellow.
We keep parakeets because of their bright colors,
so unlike the gray birds that match
our gray surroundings. Then there's the neighbor
who dyes his dog's hair in stripes of orange
to resemble a tiger. And that rock formation
looks like a woman sneering over her shoulder
or a saint in prayer, depending on who's looking.
But don't get too philosophical.
If you release the bird, it'll die in this cold.

A to Z

There is something so deeply feminine
about this pear. That's what the idiot said
right before I threw the drink on him.
Violence begets violence, the saying goes,
but love is often a one-way street.
In order to understand the product's function,
hold it to a mirror and sound out the Chinese characters.
Confusion may lead to enlightenment.
Giving birth may lead to a parallel universe
in which the only currency is lodged in the breasts.
When not on the moon, the astronaut eats space ice cream
and watches Dateline in El Paso. Living in extremes
must either be a form of disconnection or intimacy,
the dog howling as the fire truck passes.
One constant is that there will always be a Z
at the end of the alphabet. This will be pointed out
in many children's books: In Zebraland
zee zebras zest lemons and zipper zheir zooish robes
at zee end of zee day. The wind-up toy falls asleep
on my chest, heaving its feathered gears.
I've always wanted to be the softest piece
in the chess set. I've always known
there never was a soft piece in the chess set.

The Barbecue

It's tricky to step over all
the little dogs. In the neon light
the steel drum band covers
a Blondie song by the beer bin.
Guests discuss the benefits
of blind dates. Whoever said
travel is escape never met Greg.
Believe me.

The kicked rock
and then what. There is an art
to preservation that goes beyond
table manners. It involves
deviled eggs. She's pregnant
again. I could have sworn
she had her tubes tied.
Just let it go. Just eat it,
it tastes like chicken.
I shoved his tie in the air vent.
Don't tell.

Persona Poem

I'm so tired of waking up in someone else's pile
of dirty laundry. The brake light in my heart pumps
YOU it's YOU it's YOU. Mission Control sends
a robot tron to decipher the hieroglyphs
etched on my left kidney. I've been waiting
for someone to notice my incomprehensible tattoo.
Sometimes one must shout without irony
at an amusement park, It is I! St. Catherine of Assisi!
This might add meaning to one's life, obliquely.
The gravitron reminds us that we can use science
to negate physical realities, if only for five minutes
and two dollars a ride. Look at large pieces
of colored plastic for too long and they become
a metaphor for all that is wrong in the world.
Being St. Catherine of Assisi is hard in its own way.
Keeping a secret of this magnitude from my husband
could be considered a huge betrayal.
Now that St. Catherine inhabits my soul
I find it hard to be angry. My husband disappears
for a week and returns in a red Mustang convertible
with a superior sound system.
He has made some chatty girl friends and brings them in
for drinks. Sometimes life is simpler than you think.
There never was a St. Catherine of Assisi. I made that up.

Please Support the Wisconsin Guinea Pig Rescue League

I am here to be the voice for those who have been silenced
by oppressive regimes. Yesterday a warlord from an African country
torn apart by civil unrest asked me why I care about guinea pigs.
They don't do anything, he said. And they smell like shit.
I asked him what he would smell like if he were kept in a glass cage
and made to sit in his own shit. Grassroots activism is all about
starting small. Reptiles are almost never fed often enough.
And I worry about alternative energy's ability to deflate the need
for our presence in oil-rich countries in the Middle East.
What about the millions who silently put up with sub-par service
at chain restaurants? And those who calmly ignore the signs that
our ozone layer will soon make it difficult if not impossible
to establish definitively whether life exists on other planets?
I am committed to disrupting complacency. I have carried
my microscope out of the lab and into every American's home.
Please, for the sake of small animals everywhere, give generously.

The Encounter

Two nurses appear silhouetted on the hill.
They shake hands.
It's a pleasure to meet you, says Clara Barton.
Likewise, says Florence Nightingale.
There is a pause. They speak at once, then laugh.
It was hard to find the time to get away,
says Florence Nightingale.
I feel guilty already, says Clara Barton, with all
those wounded men waiting in the hospital.
A rabbit is chewing up the stalks of clover nearby.
There is the downward flash of a bird and both animals
are lifted into sky. No one flinches.
Do you believe in God? asks Florence Nightingale.
Yes, says Clara Barton.
Does everything happen for a reason?
No. Some human actions are senseless.
The two start their descent down the hill,
holding their skirts up out of the mud.
Another rabbit slowly leaves its burrow.
Are you married? asks Clara Barton.
No.
Me neither. Would you like to come over for dinner?

The Witness

There is a full moon the night St. Augustine
invents Just War Theory. Which is to say
though it is almost midnight he can see his toes,
the flowering dogwood by his door, and down
the walkway, a man beating a boy with a club.
He picks up his pen.

§

Going to Hawaii

Are we going to Hawaii?
I run to catch the beautiful speckled pigeon
you toss off the roof.
It flies, of course.
It is November, almost, and I hear the tiny skull
inside my skull.
It knocks around like a beer-nut
and makes me feel old.
Little skull, wake up!
The breakfast table blazes with a hundred strips
of sunrise. I fold the sky into quarters
and put it in my pocket for later.
Then school lets out.
I forgot about school letting out!
The kids are like wasps slowly remembering
they are wasps in springtime when mud rolls off
the hive and all the white-faced babies
come sensitive toward the fruit.
There are so many of them,
all climbing into my brain with their pincer-teeth.
It is noon and I run to catch the bacon
that is dripping off the stove in heat.
What a great surprise! It is perfect bacon!
I feed it to all the little skulls in my brain
and they begin to hum their show tunes again.
This is just how I imagined it.
Is this Hawaii?
I am so happy.

According to the Magazines, Lindsay Lohan Is Very Lonely These Days

After a meal of General Tso's, we learn
that an exciting opportunity will soon present itself.
I get up to give a toast at the wedding
but all that comes out is a gasp.
What I've learned from Hans Christian Andersen
is that there is a tiny world in each pore of the universe
populated by tiny people who also dream
of larger realities. In the space between coffee
and lunch lies an expanse as unforgiving
as a cross-country bus ride. Not knowing
where to sit or who to talk to at the barbecue,
I choose the roof. But hey, the Rubix cube
is only as hard as the guy pasting on
the colored squares wants it to be, right?
The girl who wants to be married with kids by 30
misses the point of both, no? And so the algorithm
of finding solace is the algorithm of rejecting
such algorithms in the first place.
Pirates emerge from myth. A scientist claims
to have taught a rhesus monkey to hum
the alphabet in six languages. The last baby
born in 2009 beats up the first baby born in 2010
while mothers stand by in disbelief.
The fortune-teller says grandma will trace our family
back to a happy-go-lucky seafarer from 1830s Australia.
The weatherman says life is a constant search punctuated
by tornadoes and moments of regret. I close my eyes.
It is almost my birthday. Deep in the cake

hides a plastic doll. Who put it there,
and who on earth wants to find it?

Endless Beginning

Does the war end when a piece of paper is signed?
What does the paper say, exactly?
Crocuses open at the butt crack of spring,
like the first good news, then quickly die.
Holding something more important than his body,
the messenger on horseback would ride himself
to the brink of death to get there in time.
The horse would be put out of his misery.
Now, people are born again and again
like apples rolling down an embankment
into the mouths of larger apples and so on.
Oprah says, It's the start of a new life—
Look under your seats! There's a new you
in every mirror on every door of every talk show
in your mind, and everyone's watching.
Cyberspace streams its endless reel, the tickertape
like couches after couches after couches
stretching into the longest reception area
in the world. You're last in line.
There's a tiny shadow up front, maybe a person
or a cup of coffee. What are you waiting for?
There's a riddle that shows every beginning
is just an ending tied with a bow.
I can't remember how it goes.

If You Are Lost, Don't Move

They say hysteria leads to water loss.
That post-it note in your pocket could come in handy.
Always, the most important item in your purse
is the compact mirror. At the top of the pine tree
lies another pine tree, but this one's imagined
and too high to climb. Did I say I *love you*
when I left the house today?
If you remain stationary long enough, someone
will bump into you. If you are five years old
and pretend to disappear, you will be found.
Survival is relative in certain hemispheres
of the human brain. The recipe calls for
ten gallons of maple syrup and an ingredient
you've never heard of. You are alone.
You will have to scale a gorge you didn't know existed
and leave all of your keepsakes at the bottom of the well.
No one said it would be easy. Did you pack a defibrillator?
Are you aware of how many questions will need
to be answered? All around you, nature goes on
being nature in its subtle way. You call out *me*
and it spits back *me* in a thousand dipping leaves.
Go ahead, try to ask for help.
The clouds will be whatever shape you want
as they move past.

Photo Op

The lights are flashing.
People throw flowers at my feet.
It's you! they shout.
Listen, I say. I'm here to talk about
the situation in Darfur.
Oh my God, it's you! they shout.
A girl breaks through security and faints.
All around the room people are waving
cameras and pens for autographs.
Please, please, they say. It's really you!
Just then a pigeon flies into the studio.
No one cares. A cameraman kills it with a brick.
The lights flash red, red, red.
Yay! they yell. It's you! It's you! It's really you!

The Last Time I'll Ever Do That

Want a description? There's a prescriptive
for a squirrel who loses a tail, a pot talking
to a kettle, the finale of *Weeds* in which
another hysterical woman blames herself
for sucking up tragedy through a straw.
It's a beautiful and intriguing straw, even
psychedelic. Likewise, the commercial
shows a woman escaping with a blindfold
in the back of a minivan, which is like burrowing
into a locker in the gym—no one can smell
your sweaty heart but you're still ashamed.
Thing is, most of the time no one's looking,
which is both a relief and cause for further paranoia—
no one can hear you fall like a tree in a forest
of trees with no ears. What were you doing
in a forest anyway, bro? The clip-on tie
allows for comfort while showing everyone—
what—exactly? They say getting shit on by a bird
is good luck, just like third time's a charm
or the no-strike-out rule at the picnic,
which has you swinging and swinging.
You know, the ancient purple grapes of your soul
would make some fine wine. Next time
you're near a crusher, consider it.

Dominoes

Life is mirrors pointed at other mirrors and then one day
your mom comes in and breaks them all.
She says her mother made her do it.
And her mother's mother put rocks in the soup
and tied toys too high to reach.
Nobody knew that woman's mother
but legend has it she wasn't a woman at all
but a giant prehistoric mermaid. She did her best,
but her kind was never meant to survive the treacheries
of evolution. Oh, lighten up. So your parents got divorced,
and when they fought you went outside to play
but all your toys were hanging in a net at the top of a tree,
including the transformer truck you got for your birthday,
and there was a bird making a nest in it.
Why couldn't you see any beauty in that?

A Strange Thing Happened on March 8th

All the lake-life that could swim approached shore. We could see them—the fish and the bottom dwellers and the frogs and the tiny lake worms—treading water and staring up at us, bulging, waiting. There was the pause before the speech but no speech. The rest of the lake was dark and the plants bloomed and bloomed into a forest so thick no life could swim through. They were stuck near the shore, those animals, sucking up oxygen and staring. In the end, the vertebrates and the invertebrates had to eat each other, from the smallest up until there were only a few mean fish and then they died too. Then the plants died and the lake was dark with soil and bones and the tubular remains of coontail and bladderwort. And the sun set and rose and it was March 9th and nothing had changed. Is this a parable? asked the boy. I was still grinding his knuckles into my palm. Everywhere, the world looked dark and uncertain. Let's go home, I said. It's just a sad story we can't understand.

The Machine

She has been trying for some time to connect
the umbrella to the hand crank and the hand crank
to the harmonica-induced stethoscope.
This is the last step in the perfection of the machine.
We have been waiting for years for its completion.
The inventor won't let us in the basement workroom
because it would contaminate the machine's understanding
of desire and space-time relationships.
I don't know what the machine looks like,
but I think it will take up the whole yard.
When the machine is complete, we won't need
anything else. The machine will feed us
and tuck us into bed at night. We will be amused by
the shows it will broadcast and the supersonic
speed of its amusement component.
We'll never be bored.
In a few years, we won't be able to think
of a time before we had the machine.
Life will be so simple.
There won't be any other way.

The Argument

I make a sign and you look at it.
Then you make a bigger sign.
There are exclamation points
on your sign. I use ellipses.
It took a long time to make these signs
and we are exhausted.
I drink some juice and fall asleep
on the couch. You pace around.

When I wake up, you are passed out
on the rug and the rough fiber loops
are pocking your face. It is suddenly
winter and we both seem old.

First Man Gets the Oyster, Second Man Gets the Shell

Coming from the shower, any proclamation is possible.
Just because the first domino falls
doesn't mean there will be repercussions.
Just because the children's book scares the bejesus out of me
doesn't mean I'm immature.
Every time I lace up my ice skates
there's a fire in the building. I don the hard hat
and the ski mask only to find
it's not a costume party after all. You know,
the hole in the fossil record can be attributed
to the needle-in-a-haystack phenomenon—
in other words, we're gluttons for punishment.
When I reach out for you, there's a tiny genie
in my right ear saying, Go! and an enormous
elephant in my left saying, What the fuck
are you thinking, you little shit?
I climb out of the pothole in time to see
my family disappearing in a covered wagon,
laughing and playing their pioneer games.
I order a piña colada but receive a pineapple daiquiri.
I place one foot in front of the other but find
I'm already on the moving floor.
First there was Adam and Eve, and then, well,
you know. First the largest and most comfortable bed,
then Grandma Wolf drooling in her bonnet.
I've been warned a million times, but seeing
isn't believing, it's a pit stop on the way
to somewhere else. Friday I'm at the dentist,
submitting to sharply painful logic.

Saturday I'm at the carnival, which means
I'll have another stupid chance
to win that giant panda I couldn't win
in fifth grade for Stephanie St. Clare.

Humanization Squared

I walk outside and a pinecone organized
in perfect Fibonacci sequence lands hard
on my head. The negatively charged grasses
wave around searching for positively charged
seeds. I spend all day trying to chart
the equation of my feelings but I didn't get
that far in math. The girl in little red boots
tramples over the heart-shaped meadow
in my lower abdomen. My lungs have been left
to dry in the sun. I think I deserve it.
The rock crevasse is achingly beautiful
and deeper than night. The blonde girls majoring
in communications have nothing to say about that,
or about negativity or self-doubt.
The chart in my room shows X's for each fumble
and Y's for each completed pass.
It's a meaningless jumble. Oh dishrag,
when are you not soaked in other people's scum?
Who isn't looking for the intricate equation of the universe
in CliffsNotes? In the lobby, the cheat sheet unfolds
into a murdered swan. Everyone knows
it was me. Where I thought there would be chocolate
there is a puddle of blood. Isn't it a holiday?
The waltz begins its endless, loopy necklace.
Isn't there an exit? There must be an exit.

§

The Confrontation

It is morning. Murray comes outside
carrying a machete. Put it away, I say.
He's got two little kids like pigtails
wandering over to us. I look at the kids.
Their hair is tangled. They have boogers.
I'm breaking that asshole's car, says Murray.
There is a pause. Liberation! shout the children.
The sun goes from pink to yellow like a magic trick.
I'll slash his tires! says Murray. I'll crush his mirrors!
He doesn't move. The kids are pop rocks in soda—
up and down, up and down, up and down.
Kill the beast! Eat its heart! they yell.
I look up. It's only Tuesday.
The traffic light turns from flashing red
to red, green, yellow. A neighbor
gets in his car and leaves for work.
We stand there. Murray's stomach growls.
Murray, I say. Just put it away.

I've Always Wanted to Say This

There was a time when mansions had so many rooms
they had one just for fainting. If you had to faint,
this was the best room for it—chairs the size of beds,
shag carpet, cloud-sent, the whisperings of Enya.
But when you woke up, it was the worst room in the world,
and such are the machinations of life. When I was little
I wanted to be a truck driver and now, essentially,
I'm a truck driver. I watch that show—what's it called?
I forget—for eight hours straight. Then once in a while
as I'm walking down the street, a man's eyeball pops out,
and we're both a bit surprised, and he cups it in his hands
and blows the dust off and puts it back in.
At the dinner party I tell the story of the eye popping out,
and then someone else tells about finding an ear in the gutter,
and everyone drinks more wine, and Marty finally opens up
about his little brother losing a hand in a table saw,
and Sarah admits that she once lost a nipple to a feral dog,
and Tim, after some prodding, shows the empty area
where his testicles once hung. And then we walk home and
Jesus Christ it's cold outside! says my husband, and
it's so cold it feels like something huge is about to happen,
and that's when I see both of our features slipping off
our faces and we go home anyway and make love
and rub our blank faces together and I feel a deep
and exciting newness welling up in my stomach
and I think that I *will* bake muffins tomorrow morning after all.

Hallmark Aisle

Keep looking at the leopard and it might
change its spots. Looking is not the same
as seeing, say all the get-well cards.
The deeper you go, the more in tune
are the strings on the magnificent harp
in your heart. At midnight the castles turn
to glass castles and the royalty
become rodents. They're stuck in their glass
castles, those rodents! Happy 50th!
The girl with uneven legs has to wear one heel
every day of her life, but that's nothing
compared to the quadriplegic on the Dateline
special feature. The gyroscope spins wider and wider
as it slows until it's just a hunk of purple metal
for sale at the Science Museum gift shop for $7.
Guaranteed to excite passion, reads the brochure
for the Leaning Tower of Pisa. Guaranteed
to get rid of the hiccups nine times in ten.
You and which army? taunts the bully
on the playground. Hey Peg Leg! Hey
Twinkle Toes! Nice gluteus maximus.
I think I'm falling in love
all over again, whispers the dachshund
on the greeting card. Come on, Beverly,
lose that extra pound!
Congratulations Sergey, you're a Sergeant!
Impressive sale, Dale!
In this season of disbelief may you and yours

be filled with the spirit of a hopeful sun
rising over aisle fifteen.

Nothing Is More Beautiful When You Try to Make It that Way, Joan Rivers

The celebrities are in negotiations
to sell a sex tape of their famous bodies
grinding into each other like hard candy.
Someone said you're not supposed to eat
rock candy, just look through it to see
how pink and crystallized the world becomes.
There is some truth to the old man's rant
that these days people in airports look like
raccoons crawling out of garbage cans.
Whatever happened to dignity? he asks
as he finishes the bottle of scotch.
It took a long time to get here and we're never
going back is true for any instant in time
but it feels truer every time we say it.
In order to become a titan of industry
you must begin to use social networking sites,
reads the electronic textbook on iPad. Steve Jobs,
is this what your muscular mind saw in 1971
when transcriptionists were listening to audio
and typing in their cubicles? Grandma,
you're not right about the past, but Hollywood
sure saw the future coming.
I throw the plastic dolls into the pool
but they refuse to drown. The rubber tits of women
come marching at me like the headlights
of thousands of cars fresh off the assembly line.
The last time I heard the word "mankind"
was in 2001 when Al Gore was warning
of its destruction. Yeah, yeah, say all the pundits,

climate change, salmonella, bisphenol A.
Cancer's been around since prehistoric times,
and the world's an ancient toy
in the hands of a colicky baby. Get used to it.

After a Long Day

I peel off my banana suit and enjoy
a personal dinner in front of the T.V.
It's been a long day of pulling this huge metal tractor
behind me. The boss won't tell me what it does
and I'm forced to wear a banana suit all day long.
When I get home the dog licks at my peel sadly,
and the parakeets sing me the Bob Marley song
about redemption. Why did you pick that song?
I ask, I but they just shrug and go back to cleaning
each other. As I said, I get very personal
about my dinner in front of the T.V.
This is the best part of the day.
I wouldn't change this moment for the world.

Retrospect

Up close it turns out she is not my mother.
The painting is not a painting but a meticulous assemblage
of brushstrokes cut and pasted to form the shawl
of the emigrant. She's huddling—no, she's holding something—
someone. Breasts like Indian burial mounds. Ears like embryos.
All those eighties fight songs on the team bus congeal
into the ultimate fight song: it's a shriek
only dogs can hear. No one appreciates my sauce
from the can these days, not even Fido.
No one appreciates the black and whiteness
of the woodblock print. The red and blueness
of the razor nick. The stuffed panda with the bikini
I didn't win at the fair last weekend. The beads
I never made into a necklace for your birthday.
I wish I could express how much I think about
my best intentions every morning as I rinse off
my shower gel and pick the lint from between my toes.
Yet all the pin numbers in the world added together
still couldn't reach Pi, couldn't touch the level
of my fondness for you. Think how many stitches
there are in a sweater, how much sheep hair
in a thread, how much DNA in a hair, how much hair
in the world. How many paintings of hair, how much hair
covered by shawls and swept into the dust bin
at the hairdresser. All that hair! All that love!
When the weather icon on the laptop goes *pkaw*
it might be time to reassess the options,
to clean the grime from the beautiful iron ashtray
of my heart. Ask the dust bunnies what it means

to get old. I sprinkle your ashes
all over your favorite place
which is also my favorite place.

The Great Wide Open

In the Russian film there are an agonizing thirty minutes
shot in Siberia. In the Japanese film there are an agonizing
thirty minutes shot in Siberia. Who won?
The snow is not a metaphor. How easy it would be
to die here, says the Japanese film, shivering.
I hand it my wool blanket. Don't give up, I say.
No one would want that. What is it to want?
asks the Japanese film. What is it to be missed?
I lied about the snow. It is the largest white bird
stuffing you into her nest. The churches line up
on Main Street, small to large, like graded eggs.
Their bells play the same summons:
Guilty Guilty Guilty or Love Love Love
depending on who's listening.
Those crazed militiamen used to be the boys next door,
rolling up the block on big wheels. It has been said
the acclaimed poet never surpassed the poem he wrote in 1973.
I told you so, says the Russian film. Destiny
is a frail buffalo taking you into the tundra.
But small, white animals live there, with hardly
any needs at all. There is so little to learn from them.
The films fade into oblivion, leaving me
stranded. The world refuses to cough up
what I wished for all those years with my pennies.
The emptiness magnifies my importance
then snatches it back like a kid.
So this is what it's like in the Great Wide Open.
So this is what they meant.

The Ascent

Through the bars I see the silent ladies
pick tulips. A pigeon mistakes its own shit
for something else. I become noticed
then vanish again. I accept the diagnosis.
Still, I'd like a breakfast burrito
with my coffee, nurse. When I say
I don't believe in predictions it means
all my regrets are on backorder.
I've been watching myself from across the room
for thirty years. I'd ask you to dance
but I've lost all motor skills in my mouth.
Tijuana, when did you get so paunchy?
Ladies, won't you speak?
I turn on the T.V. and Lisa slaps Johnny hard.
Change the channel and a nature show
lets me know we can't see most living things.
I hold up a magnifying glass and something fizzles.
The manifestation of my desires?
Nah. The self-help video says
to picture yourself on top of a mountain
you have created amidst the applause
of everyone who didn't believe in you.
I unfold the aging love note and discover
a small man in formal wear who tells me
to stop reminiscing. Halfway down the slide,
try not to get rubber burn. Halfway up the ladder,
hey, you've still got half a ladder left.

How I Wrote a Belated Love Letter

Hold this yellow boxing glove
that has found its way into the form
of a tulip petal. Imagine it is the last thing
I will ever give you in confidence.
If we stand in a circle we reach a unity
that comes with the impersonal.
A rhino dies in Sudan, and a little boy
dies in Waco. Over the din
a piccolo announces itself.
People say things without knowing
whether they will come
to fruition. Instead of a baby,
I found a candy wrapper in my bed.
I wanted to tell you in February
but now it is May and all I have left
is this boxing glove. It is the same yellow
as the crest of my imaginary cockatiel.
I hold the cockatiel in my hands like a candle
and it tells me to think about
what happened last year in Florida.
I don't want to think about what happened
last year in Florida. Do you?

A Tediously Slow Realization

Somewhere in Scotland the lambs crest a hill
and head back down. The lemmings jump.
When I acted that way, it was on behalf of the species.
That's how come I got bruised knees, swear.
Weatherman says 49% chance of sun,
49% chance of rain, 2% chance of nothing at all.
Scientists are still interpreting the results of all non-numerical
equations such as why when asked to draw
their dream house, most people in Hawaii
will add a chimney with springs of smoke.
Wake up, grandma, the song's on repeat.
I've been trying all day to fit this square block
into this round hole. I've been trying to remember all those lessons
in morality. In mortality. Philosophy will save us all.
Make that religion. Make that two eggs over easy,
no salt, with a side of fresh greens. The only escape
is realizing you're already there, or as my father
likes to say, Wherever you go, there you are.
After a fitful night, I wake up massaging
the feet of my enemy. The idea sweats droplets
of itself all over my skull. Internet, I don't hate you.
America, I don't hate you. I never wanted it
but now I wipe my forehead with your bandanna.
Aw, hell. It smells sweeter than I would have thought.

The First Law of Thermodynamics

All across America, men are inventing
the steam engine while women sew
the faces of presidents into quilts.
If a whistle is left alone in the forest
it may restore a measure of silence
to the world. Television
reminds me of a math problem
I got wrong on the SAT. Come on, Kathy says,
can't you just enjoy it for once? By now we know
who patented the steam engine,
but think of all the men who tinkered around,
helping to invent it. Kathy is like one
of their wives, knitting a scarf
out of peach wool. Kathy, I say,
feeling a burst of goodwill,
I'll give you all my collectibles.
Thanks, she says. I'll take the John Lennon
dinnerware set for eight. As I walk home
to get it, the world looks like
a Brueghel painting and all the trees
are sending off beautiful
little equations into the air.

So Much Beauty from Despair

We've lived in the snow and the ice for so long
that when the crocuses come we turn our heads.
I fold the napkin into a crane
but it remains stationary.
This morning my shoes were all
one size too big, so turns out I've been
overestimating the size of my feet for years.
Apparently I'm no good at live-band karaoke
nor can I tie a decent knot. The train comes
and leaves and there I am on the platform
in a tutu, oversized ballet shoes around my neck.
As I stand on the deserted platform
all the young athletes run by with their water bottles.
I remember the time I had the champion pig
in fifth grade. It is a sad but lovely moment.
I eat the pistachios in my pocket.
The next train comes and leaves.
I extricate the chopsticks from my purse.
A girl enters stage right with a flute
and I can feel the crescendo building.
A three-legged cat with no fur paws by.
I toss my ballet shoes from center stage
and crumple dramatically. The audience explodes.
Then it's over and a sad monkey with a cap
starts picking up the pistachio shells.
I decide to give the monkey a good home.
He sits on my shoulder and is very pleased.
We will stop for bananas on the way back,
I tell him. He claps his hands and begins
to clean the wax out of my ear.

THE AUTHOR

LAUREN SHAPIRO received a BA in Comparative Literature from Brown University and an MFA in Poetry from the Iowa Writers' Workshop. She is a former associate acquiring editor at the Yale University Press and has translated poetry from Spanish, Italian, Vietnamese, and Arabic into English. She is the author of a chapbook, *Yo-Yo Logic* (DIAGRAM / New Michigan Press, 2012), and her poems have been published in such journals as *Pool*, *Passages North*, *32 Poems*, *Forklift, Ohio*, *Drunken Boat*, *notnostrums*, and *Thermos*. She is a curator of the Monsters of Poetry Reading Series and an assistant editor at Rescue Press. She lives with her family outside of Hartford, Connecticut.